"Abe" by Charles Haywood Johnson

FOR LINCOLN

& OTHER POEMS

by Austin Alexis

POETS WEAR PRADA · HOBOKEN, NJ

FOR LINCOLN

First North American Publication 2010.

Grateful acknowledgment is made to the following publications where some of these poems have previously appeared or will soon appear:

Brownstone Poets Anthology, Chopin with Cherries: A Tribute in Verse (Moonrise Press), *Empty Shoes: Poems on the Hungry and the Homeless* (Popcorn Press), *Ginosko, In Other Words* (Western Reading Series, 2005, Denver, Colorado), Marymark Press *Give-Out Sheet Series, Nomad's Choir, Ocean Diamond, Poetz.com, RogueScholars.com,* and *Shabdaguchha.*

ISBN 978-0-9841844-3-9

Printed in the U.S.A.

Cover Art: "Drop Drop," mixed-media montage, 2010, Roxanne Hoffman

Title Illustration: "Abe," ink on paper, 2010, Charles Haywood Johnson

Back Cover Author Photo: Marisa Train, Olan Mills Portrait Studios

For Lincoln

Contents

CHOPIN AND SAND
for Frederic Chopin, 1810-1849

A man coughing up blood
on a white keyboard.
A woman taking care of him.
A woman adding a man
to her case, her collection
and at last having something to do,
a person who becomes an activity.

He lives in her shawl.
He lives on her shelf.
She frowns, afraid he might chip
or crack in two or scar.
He lives in her nest.
She is all leaves.
She is plenty of twigs.

His fingers sing for her;
they chirp; they fly.
She is the maple his claws grip,
the branch he needs
in order to soar.

He desires her as she longs for him.
They are as far apart
as petals of a single rose.

HAYDN'S SYMPHONY
for Franz Joseph Haydn, 1732-1809

A watch is ticking, ticking...
Huge time moves minutely through
reality, and helps create it.
Hear it tock   inch   creep
like the overgrown clock in Haydn's symphony
or an elephant's booming steps
imprinting themselves on the world.
Time is that kind of dinosaur.

Each second is inextinguishable.
Every half-minute is a muscular thrust —
the triumph of a tidal wave.
All the world is a tempo
revved-up, speeding and imposing itself
like a symphony invading a lullaby.

POE'S BROOKLYN
Edgar Allan Poe, 1809-1849

Peering across the East River toward Brooklyn
his heart aflutter,
Poe saw or imagined he saw
ravens ravenous
as they swooped-down for a worm or bug
slithering and crawling in the Brooklyn thickets.

And projecting beyond the bush country
we now call Bushwick
he saw or hallucinated
automatons in the graveyards,
those misty stretches
so plentiful and spacious in Brooklyn,
spotted with gray rectangles of death
even as Poe's dead arose
savior-like and monstrous.

Poe must have longed to row
or take a ferry over
to see his Gothic vocabulary in action:
the shadows of Flatbush
elongated in moonlight
along earth of unending horizontals
capable of gobbling up anyone —
even Poe himself —
in a premature burial
perfect as a death wish that's granted.

POE'S SISTER

Outside the home for indigents
she, like a forerunner of bag ladies,
wrapped in rags and pride,
haunted Baltimore streets
a woman of letters
with a book or two of his
and his face printed on parchment
clutched in her hand.

SCENE

He tries to sell his poetry
on the street.
He wants to share his lines.
He strives and strives.

He sets up a card table
where he displays this poem and that,
each verse a fetus
waiting to be born
in the heart of a reader.

By day, by dusk, in fog, in chill,
at this corner and that,
he sits with his work.
Sometimes a sale;
sometimes an almost-sale.
His words enclosed in folders.
The poet wrapped in a worn overcoat.
All of them encased
in a picture, a tableau entitled
the loneliness of art.

AT THE MARTHA GRAHAM STUDIO

Probing for a resting place
my back moves back, progressively back
until it reaches a firm softness.
Good. Now, resting in a studio nest
I watch the dance concert,
   the dancers' energy eagerly flying,
   just short of frantic,
   their chests heaving with fire.

During intermission's stream
a fellow audience member floats to me,
touches me on my shoulder,
a mild gravity in her stroke.
"You're leaning on Martha's legs," she whispers
in a calm voice that waves a warning.

I spiral behind myself to peek,
view for the first time
vulnerability in Martha's expression.
And indeed I had been
carelessly, without rancor or even intent,
using the sacred legs as a rest —
tarnishing the image of the goddess.

FOR MERCE CUNNINGHAM

The wire man's voltage
springs alive, active, even agitated.
It experimentally probes
humid dance air, tests theories,
penetrates the impenetrable questions,
the mysteries of space   time   weight.

In a building flanking a river
he moves though standing
bolted to one rectangular place.
A summer space.
A wintry branch, tossed
yet trained to its firm bark.
Stream-like is his swift pace.
River-like is his steadfast movement.

In his sparse/cluttered loft
at night he rests.
He sits back, is finished lunging at dancers,
barking orders at cabdrivers,
watching the secret movement of plants
that jungle his stage-high windows.
At home he is a macaw
calmly theatrical
stationed in a rainforest.
Alert to relaxation, he putters
like a beach bird
amid a gift of holiday litter.

When time to sleep arrives on cue
he catches its rhythm
in his unique way.
See his Einstein hairs poking like limbs
through midnight air.
See his electric fingers
twitching as he dreams.

PARK LADY

To go from a slope of black dirt
to waiting brown water
is her objective:
a bath in wintry Central Park.
The pond beckons with its city ducks
and nautical sewer rats.
This place is better than nothing.

She doesn't bother to undress.
Let the plastic garbage bags she has patiently
fashioned into blouse and skirt
bell around her like a nimbus.
Let the paper bags she uses for shoes
soak and tear in the pond's moist throat.

After her dip she will rest,
lounge upon boulders west of the water.
She will pat herself dry
before a dinner party with the pigeons.

GONE

You are missing...
erased from paper,
leaving only a smudge
for others to contemplate.

Your peering children
lunge into a void
fishing, fishing for you.
You do not bite their bait.

You've become a black duck
drifting on a night lake,
both of you too dark
to be seen —

only heard:
whispered striving of waves,
isolated squawks,
pauses, hollow with silence.

HER ROOM

My grandma's room heaved
with the furnace of sickness,
a wall, a bellowing of heat —
illness touchable and long-lasting.
Her perfume bottles — a glass tower city —
sprawled on her dresser,
sweated through a sticky heat wave
generated by her forehead, neck and chest
under duress of fever
and fear and wet-heavy multiplying blankets.
A sad tropical body.
A sad tropical land, her room.
The odor of a requiem
lingered in the moist red drapes,
their languid folds — the old worn cloth —
solemn as a sunset.

GRANDPA

You talked to yourself
and shuffled like an old man
years before you were elderly.

You arrived places on big-clown bozo feet,
back slightly forward as if weighed down
by your secret sack of pennies.

You exiled your wife's dog
to the hot tar roof of a garage,
casual cruelty being your style.

You gifted your grands with silver dollar coins —
stars to glow in their pockets —
kindness gracing your checklist.

You protected your skin, your health
with mega-naps on a couch
as large as many a pre-war bedroom.

You shielded yourself
with stern silences
and eyes that looked at no one.

You took in plenty through prominent ears,
those usually wax-packed canals
that didn't care to hear.

You let one long clear tear etch
down your cheek
when your son couldn't stop dying.

You passed away when you felt like it
in the cloister of your railroad flat,
a monk till the end.

INSOMNIAC

I am the screech in silence.
Also the quiet
that is too insistent.
During still night, my long hours
long not to be so long.
Like the prematurely buried
I can't stay put — nor rise.
All options seem impossible
though they tease.
Stray thoughts chaos my mind.
Held hostage, my mind rebels against
the hush that would free it.

I am a vase that has fractured.
When all three thousand pieces
are found and reassembled
I'll sleep.

PUZZLE

When Albert Einstein stuck his tongue out
for the camera
was it clean?
And if he didn't care,
why not?
What equation was he mucking-up,
what Inca cord math was he unknotting,
or what graph was he scribbling upon
by defiantly not washing his mouth?
What proof
was he trying to prove?
Did he always have a pronouncement?
Was he saying
with his lips gaping
like a Rocky Mountain cave
that the mysteries of X,
the nagging questions of existence
are too profound
for seriousness?

THE SUBWAY JOKER

When you slipped
and your leg plunged
into a dark indentation
between the train and the walkway
you looked up and smirked
like a TV comedian
who'd delivered his best one-liner.

The subway car passengers
didn't find the incident so laughable.
Some of them cried out;
others turned their heads,
not wanting to witness
the wicked seconds
they felt sure would follow.

Had the train started up
while your body remained
half on the platform
half in the hole
you would have been a disaster,
split in two maybe,
perhaps decapitated.

But you sprang out of that gap,
found comfort in a subway seat
then nonchalantly looked around,
ignoring how micro-close
you had inched toward
a nightmare as finale.

As if you'd won a game
by skillfully cheating,
your lips lengthened horizontally;
your vertical teeth glowed.
You lived, attempting the grin of ignorance,
signaling without meaning to
all you wish you didn't know.

EYELASHES

We curve upward.
A prototype of grace, if we could sing:
what rhapsodies!
But instead we gesture, attractive in our shapeliness.
Like tiny arms
no, feathers   wings
we interact with wind and light.
Sunlight plays upon our delicious figures,
wants to eat our minuteness
and feel sated.

Our misleading delicateness handles
the scrub of face-washing,
harsh chemicals of mascara.
Only hair, nonetheless we survive,
bounce back when pressed down,
angel-soft
yet resilient as healthy tendons,
tough as strands of steel wool.

THE DROP

He just happened to be there,
his timing Mozart-perfect,
the slate sidewalk
more sacred than a shrine.

The baby came plunging
from a crane-high windowsill
down   down   irreversible
as water spiraling a drain.
She tumbled — a huge raindrop
ready to splash
or a chunk of hail
speeding toward oblivion.

His head tilted upward
at that exact beat
to see the infant dancer
on her waltz toward death.

Had he not caught a green light
moments earlier...
Had he not
casually stopped
to button his sweater
at that spot...
Had luck's directions
been a fraction less honed...

But he was there —
Samson or Hercules —
stationed there by time,
and his arms stretched out
in a pope-like gesture
to break the fated fall
as the laws of nature
hold the hovering moon in the sky.

The moment glowed
for him and for the baby.
That second was a shock,
then a grin,
then became a promenade
featuring Destiny strutting,
wearing bells around its ankles.

FOR LINCOLN
(1809-1865)

I.

Your old-man skin
worn on your
young-man posture
in a youthful country
about to grow up fast.

II.

You went to the theatre
not knowing
and not wanting to know.

All that red velvet!
And you didn't pay heed
to the color.

III.

What suit, what formality
did your wife package you in
as she, understandably, unraveled...

IV.

The memorial pictures you
with monumental hands,
eyes eying the land,
and a huge face
housing a subtle smile.

ELECTION AFTERNOON, ELECTION EVENING

I have to admit there are times
I can't stand life
and this is one of them:
this stretch of eight hours
from 3 p.m. through 11:00 p.m.
as the election results
straddle a trembling tightrope.
Suspense has never been my friend
and today it's psyched-up —
as sadistic as a novelist
torpedoing her characters' lives.
Today my life is wounded
by a friend's telephone calls
every twenty minutes
detailing the states Obama is losing:
West Virginia, Arkansas, Tennessee.
"Oh no!" my friend cries
as she eyes CNN's election charts.
Does she know she's torturing my ears
or is she simply enjoying
a bit of self-flagellation?

After several such calls
I want to say
and finally do say
"Don't give me the blow-by-blow.
I can't take it. My heart...
It would be too icky if he loses,"
and similar cry-baby words.
We hang up.

I look at my silent radio,
my mute TV,
and thank them for their cooperation.
But then staccato news-journalist voices
assault me from two back yards away.
I can't hear distinct words
just an urgency of language

I know could only be about
Obama, McCain, McCain, Obama.
I close my apartment windows,
retreat to my kitchen area
and slip a Debussy cassette
into my kitchen boom-box.
Oh, the blessings of electronics.

I cook dinner, floating
in serene aromas
for a while,
until anxiety trumps Debussy
like cancer outdoing chemotherapy.
"If I'm a wreck, imagine poor Barack,
put-upon Michelle.
They must be in hell," I say aloud
to the faucet and can-opener.
But then I acknowledge they might be
sipping champagne
and leafing through catalogues
for new White House carpets.

I try but fail to calm myself
by eating and reading,
reading and eating,
asparagus and Updike to no avail.
But, after a long-short while,
when I hear a roar of joy
lifting from the apartment below mine
I know it's possible to turn on the radio
without jitters.
I do so.
An announcer proclaims the winner
several times
as if his words are a song
he can't s top chanting.

I turn-off the kitchen light.
I leisurely floss
and take my radio to bed.

INAUGURATION

You stood tall,
grew taller.
No ceiling existed.

Your hand touched the Bible —
a drumstick
tapping out an anthem.

You planned to rule
without throne,
no crown on your mind.

Your regal voice
managed humble notes
that confettied the air.

Acknowledgments

Poems in this volume have been published or are scheduled to appear, sometimes in different versions, in the following journals and anthologies. To the editors, thanks are due.

"Chopin and Sand" *Chopin with Cherries: A Tribute in Verse,* edited by Maja Trochimczyk (Moonrise Press, 2010)

"Election Afternoon, Election Evening" *Poetz.com*

"Eyelashes" *Ginosko*

"For Merce Cunningham" Marymark Press *Give-Out Sheet Series*

"Gone" *Nomad's Choir*

"Grandpa" *Brownstone Poets Anthology*

"Haydn's Symphony" *Nomad's Choir*

"Her Room" *In Other Words,* (Western Reading Series, 2005, Denver, Colorado)

"Insomniac" *RogueScholars.com*

"Park Lady" *Empty Shoes: Poems on the Hungry and the Homeless* (Popcorn Press, 2009)

"Poe's Brooklyn" *Shabdaguchha; Brownstone Poets Anthology*

"Poe's Sister" *Ocean Diamond* (print and on-line)

Thanks also to Rose Alexis, Patricia Carragon, Peter Chelnik, Roxanne Hoffman, and Elaine Shipman.

About the Author

Poems and stories by Austin Alexis have appeared in journals such as *Six Sentences* and *Tuesday Shorts* and in the chapbook *Lovers and Drag Queens* (Poets Wear Prada, 2007). Recently he served as a panelist for The Bronx Council on the Arts Literary Fellowships. One of his poems won a prize in the 2008 Poets for Forest Competition.

His work has appeared or is forthcoming in a number of anthologies, including *Bowl of Stories* (Oregon Council of Teachers Anthology Winners Publication), *Off the Cuffs* (Soft Skull Press), *Dinner with the Muse* (Ra Rays Press), *Art's Buoyant Felicity: Art/Healing/Creativity* (Lickle Nine Press), and *And We the Creatures* (Dream Horse Press), among others.

About the Illustrator

Charles Haywood Johnson, fine artist, has documented the interior garden court of The Frick, the high altar and pulpit of the Cathedral Church of St. John the Divine, and the Children's Portico at the Pratt Institute Library which is a replica of the Boys' Entranceway at Canterbury, England.

Also by Austin Alexis

Lovers and Drag Queens (Poets Wear Prada, 2007)

www.ingramcontent.com/pod-product-compliance
Lightning Source LLC
Chambersburg PA
CBHW061759040426
42447CB00011B/2382